Old DALKEITH

by
Rhona Wilson

THE LAST BUS. FROM WAVERLEY TO DALKEITH

WE ALL GO THE SAME WAY HOME.

© Stenlake Publishing 1997
First Published in the United Kingdom, 1997,
by Stenlake Publishing,
Telephone / Fax: 01290 551122

ISBN 1 872074 80 4

The publishers regret that they cannot supply
copies of any pictures featured in this book.

DALKEITH.

Dalkeith's motto is 'Once the Guardians, Always the Defenders' (of the crown) and refers both to the role it played within the feudal system, and the Scottish regalia that, according to the records of 1639, was housed at the castle. The version of Dalkeith's Coat of Arms shown here was an unofficial one, adopted in the 1880s and abandoned on the order of the Lord Lyon King of Arms in 1930.

INTRODUCTION

Blaeu's 1607 Map of Scotland shows Dalketh (sic) clearly bounded by the North and South Esk, illustrating one of the possible derivations of its name; the Celtic 'dal' meaning 'a dale' and 'caeth' meaning 'confined'. However, the *Third Statistical Account* (published in the 1950s) states that the consensus was that the name Dalkeith came from the Gaelic 'dail-catha', meaning 'field of battle'. The village was never a particular focus for combat, but it is thought that this sinister derivation may have arisen during the feudal period of Scottish history. In 1547, fugitives from the Battle of Pinkie (waged against the English), were reputedly massacred in the fields surrounding the burgh, their graves uncovered by labourers in 1888 This latter theory has been discreditied with most scholars citing the Celtic derivation.

Dalkeith Castle was first documented by the French historian Froissart in the early fourteenth century but, along with the village, it is thought to have existed long before then. The Grahams were its first traceable feudal lords, holding the lands for two hundred years. The properties then passed onto the Douglases through marriage, and it was under their ownership that Dalkeith was made into a Burgh of Barony by Robert III in 1401. However, bad housekeeping on the Douglases part meant that the lands passed to the Buccleuch family in 1642. However William, 7th Earl of Morton spent so much money proving his loyalty to Charles I that he had to sell his assets, Dalkeith included.

Dalkeith's status as a burgh entitled it to rights and privileges of trade which the town quickly developed. One of the largest grain markets in Scotland was held weekly in the High Street, the ready-money trading attracting suppliers and buyers from far afield. In 1718, the Duchess of Buccleuch owned over 2,500 acres of farm land, with oats the main crop. During the first half of the eighteenth century vast improvements were made to the land, encouraged by the Duke of Buccleuch who introduced drainage systems on his tenants' land for free (although for his own benefit as much as theirs, no doubt). Simple agricultural principles such as crop rotation were used to increase yields, resulting in Dalkeith 'rejoicing under glorious crops of potatoes', according to one writer. The swelling food supply heralded the beginning of population rises, as well as increasing the wealth of the district. In 1801 Dalkeith's population was just under 4,000, fifty years later it had risen to over 6,500.

By the mid-nineteenth century the industrial revolution was also making its presence felt in Dalkeith. Disparate industries such as the iron foundry, gas works, brewery, tannery and builders all sprung up. Several banks were established in the town (including the Commercial, National and Royal) to take care of the community's burgeoning wealth. However, others could only invest themselves in the Poor House, which existed until 1838 and was only abolished because there was no demand for the labour of its forty odd inhabitants. Communications also developed rapidly, and the Edinburgh and Dalkeith Railway opened in 1831. Although originally intended as a goods service, it recovered its costs by transporting passengers.

Over the centuries, Dalkeith's local government was transformed. From 1760 to 1878 the town was run by twelve trustees, who raised funds by a local tax on beer. Appointed for life, with successors chosen by those remaining, the system was hardly democratic. Critical leaders in the *Dalkeith Advertiser* regarding the trustees' management (particularly of the water supply) in the late 1860s testify to the movement against them. In 1878 reformers succeeded in getting Dalkeith declared a police burgh, allowing it to elect its own council. At this point Dalkeith also expanded in size. The Old Town, concentrated around High Street and Back Street, was supplemented by a residential district at Eskbank circa the 1880s. A further housing drive took place in the inter-war years of the twentieth century when the Shadepark, Gibralter, Elmfield and lower Woodburn schemes were built, creating around 650 houses.

The period from the late 1800s to the turn of the twentieth century saw huge changes affect Dalkeith. Agriculture ceased to be of such importance, and the famous grain market died out. In the 1950s coal mining was cited as the most important source of employment in the area at a time when its demise was being charted in the west of Scotland. Dalkeith actually brought miners in from Lanarkshire at this period, as if it had been saving this resource for a rainy day! Many of the old industries had closed down, although some such as the brewery and the brush factory (established in High Street in 1779) survived for a time. Transport too had changed dramatically with the railway succumbing to buses in the early 1940s.

Today Dalkeith is a curious mixture of the charming and the modern. Although much of the Old Town is intact, and features such as the Water Tower have been preserved, a substantial area to the south of High Street has been redeveloped. Flats and government offices now occupy this area, as well as the glorious Jarnac Shopping Precinct, completed in 1965. The removal of overcrowded and unsanitary closes and wyndes precipitated its erection, but that hardly seems an excuse for the monstrous concrete block left squatting in their place.

Recently, the main local issue in Dalkeith has been the perennial traffic problem. Town inhabitants were angling for a bypass to ease congestion until they were granted their wish on condition the road went slam through the palace grounds. This is still a relevant issue since the by-pass has been accepted in principle but is awaiting funding. The park and palace remain intact and Dalkeith is a pleasant dormitory town full of the comfortable homes of professionals.

Dalkeith, photographed from the High Woods in 1909. West Church (later Buccleuch) appears on the right of this panoramic view, with the spire of St Nicholas's Church visible on the left. Dalkeith Grammar School was situated behind St Nicholas's Church . Dating from the late seventeenth century, it was the only school in the parish at one point. When it was first established, the school provided a classical education before broadening its remit to encompass more familiar subjects (mathematics and geography, for example) later on. Although it only had a small number of pupils they were an illustrious class indeed, going on to powerful posts in their later careers, several becoming Lord High Chancellors, Lord Provosts or just plain Lords. It is thought by some commentators, however, that children from poorer families would also have had the chance to attend lessons there.

This 1909 picture shows the fields where sheep and cattle would be penned for the adjoining auction market; afterwards the animals were taken to the nearby slaughter house. The scene is very different today since, from the late 1960s, the fields were increasingly encroached upon by buildings.

Bridgend Toll House (photographed *c.*1910) was designed and positioned to discourage cheats. It was circular to ensure that potential customers could be seen approaching from all angles, and placed at a junction so that there was no way a traveller could skulk in or out of town by a back route. Before the arrival of turnpikes in the eighteenth century, roads were unmaintained dirt tracks. Originally collected by the Duke of Buccleuch's office, the Edinburgh Road toll revenue would have been used for road and bridge maintenance; later this became the responsibility of the Turnpike Trustees who built the Toll House around 1804. Tolls were abolished in 1883 and the house was demolished in 1946. A small garden plot now occupies the site with a garage and flats behind it.

Bridgend photographed from the Edinburgh Road, 1911. The building to the left with crow-stepped gables was the house at the burgh slaughterhouse. Dalkeith's butchers seem to have been a strange and unpopular breed: as far back as 1766 the town trustees called a meeting to try to dissuade them from their particularly nasty habit of slaughtering animals in the street instead of using the common 'Killing House' between Back Street and High Street. However, the butchers claimed that the building was overcrowded and overtaken by women and children for hanging out washing and playing in. Complaints against the butchers persisted and the council eventually acquired the site at Bridgend in 1901, with the Co-op having the dubious honour of slaughtering the first cow when it was completed three years later. The abattoir closed around the 1950s when it was considered to be unhygienic and inefficient with the building being taken over as council offices. The site was eventually redeveloped as housing in the 1970s.

Bridgend, Dalkeith.

Taken in 1903, this picture shows most of Bridgend. In February 1911 there was scandal when thirteen guests at a whist party in Bridgend were poisoned by the after-dinner coffee. Arsenic was found to be the culprit for the two deaths (Mr Hutchinson, the host, and Mr Clapperton, a Musselburgh merchant), and two weeks after the incident the police were hot on the heels of John Hutchinson, the elder son of the household, who'd fled to Guernsey as suspicions arose regarding him. Hutchinson was generally known as a bad egg (gambling, impregnation and stock exchange flirtations being a few of his hobbies) and it seems his haphazard plan was to use his father's life insurance to pay off his debts, estimated at around £8,000. The sorry affair ended when he was confronted by detectives and chose to swallow a phial of prussic acid rather than be taken into custody, dying soon afterwards.

All the buildings in this 1905 picture of Bridgend have been demolished, except for the Lugton Inn (in the background). This hostelry has had a varied history and was once called the Plough Inn, before being reborn as The Log Cabin, a wild west theme pub which, unsurprisingly, didn't last for long. Due to subsidence on the main road a few years ago, traffic had to be diverted through the village of Lugton for a time.

Dalkeith Fish Restaurant at 104 High Street was once owned by B. Cavaroli. Later it became Youngs and then Smiths, before ending up as The Cavalier Restaurant.

Dalkeith Co-op was founded in 1861 and had its first shops in High Street before moving to this grand building – known locally as the People's Palace – in 1888. These premises, situated at the junction of Lothian Street and Newmills Road, were arranged around a central court and included stables, a grocery (seen on the corner), bakery, iron mongers, and millinery and drapery departments. Upstairs there were workshops and stores for the different sections. In 1915 its assets were transferred to Musselburgh and Fisherrow Co-operative Society, and with its failing fortunes the building was sold to Dalkeith Town Council in 1968. However, the Co-op was active for another twenty years in Dalkeith, not closing its branch at Eskdaill Court until 1988.

Dalkeith Hospital. Fear of fever was rife in the nineteenth century town, and in 1831 a Board of Health with the power to inspect households was formed for the prevention of cholera. Records dating from 1882 speak of an extension to the building to provide accommodation for patients with infectious and non-infectious diseases. However, as early as 1894 the County Sanitary Inspector expressed concerns that it wasn't good enough. Farcical disaster occurred in 1908 when scarlet fever and diphtheria broke out in Dalkeith at the same time; patients afflicted by the latter couldn't be moved to the hospital because it posed such a threat of cross-infection. In 1910 the Duke of Buccleuch offered land at Whitehill for a new hospital and the Cottage Hospital closed in 1913.

The 'New Hospital', Dalkeith, replaced the earlier cottage hospital. This postcard was sent in July 1918.

Bonnyrigg Road with Muirpark on the right in 1908. Henry Widnell and Stewart's carpet factory, now demolished, once stood nearby. The factory was originally built in the late 1870s, as a branch of an enterprise set up by Richard Whytock around forty years earlier in Edinburgh. Whytock experimented with a patterning technique for carpets whereby threads were dyed different colours throughout their length resulting in an instant pattern when woven. The effect was called 'tapestry carpet' and proved very successful. During World War II Ever Ready took over the premises to produce batteries as part of the war effort. The buildings on the right behind the lamp-post have now gone, the church replaced by an ESSO petrol station.

CROSS ROADS, ESKBANK.

R.R.R.
E.

A corner of Old Station Road, looking back towards the toll. The open space behind the road has now been built on.

Dalkeith once had six oatmeal and two flour mills although by the 1950s only one, A. & W. Douglas Mill (established in 1835 and selling 'Dalkeith Meal') survived. One of the corn mills was called the Iron Mill because it was previously used to produce iron bars and sheet iron, the hammers being raised by water power. The mill was owned by James Gray at the time and only converted to its new use when the iron business declined. There are a couple of reasons cited for the demise of the flour trade – mainly that people became less dependent on oats as a foodstuff. The Elginhaugh flour mills on the North Esk (above) are disused but still standing.

Motel Derry on the road to Hawick from Eskbank Toll around 1965, featuring some classic 60s cars. There is a Fiat 600 and beside that an Austin 1100, one of the most popular cars in the UK in the late 1960s, although few survive today. Next in line is a Ford Zodiac with a Vauxhall VX4/90 and a Mini at the end on the right.

Eskbank Road, Dalkeith.

Except for the Harrow Hotel (in the foreground), all the buildings on the right hand side of this picture of Eskbank Road, taken from the junction of Buccleuch Street, have gone. The new post office and offices of the Eastern Scottish bus company now stand on their site. Formerly home to a grocers, a bank, and Adams the butcher (famous for his Dalkeith Sausages), the left side of the road is now host to not one but two funeral parlours, followed by a flower shop. Beside that is the St John and Kings Park Church.

T. Wallace, the enterprising Dalkeith photographer, managed to get both the royal visitors and his shop-front in this picture of Eskbank Road taken in August 1907. Meticulous preparations went on weeks in advance of the arrival of the then Prince and Princess of Wales (later George V and Queen Mary). A triumphal archway was erected at the head of the High Street, the town decorated and games organised in the park for the children granted a day off school. Councillors even found time to dither about whether or not to lay down sand in the streets (so the visitors' royal feet didn't have to touch the pavements) since it had been such a bother to clear up after previous visits. The royal couple stayed at Dalkeith Palace, joining a long list of historic guests. The Palace (converted from a castle in the early 1700s) has long ceased to have a royal role or even be used as a residency and is now a branch of the University of Wisconsin.

Eskbank Toll in 1908, showing evidence of a gentler pace of life. Lasswade Road looks straight ahead to a tree-filled scene, now built up. The chemist on the left is now an antique shop while Foreman's grocers is now empty and may be demolished.

The same scene, photographed in 1911 as Provost Tod unveils an ornamental fountain. Eskbank Toll, known locally as 'Galla's Ha'' (Gallow's Halt), was the meeting point for six roads and would have been a stopping point for a lot of thirsty horses.

This picture, taken in 1955, shows the extent of the remodelling at Eskbank Toll. The rather primitive signpost has gone, replaced by a roundabout. The Bank of Scotland branch, behind the Fordson van, has also gone. At around the same time the Savings Bank would have had premises in Eskbank Road. This started from an offshoot of the Scientific Society, established in 1835. The savings branch was set up four years later and by its centenary had received over £200,000 worth of deposits.

Bonnyrigg Road, Eskbank   No. 5943

Cockburn and Sons ran taxis and a bus known as 'Cobbie's Bus' which did the Cockpen Circular, a route to Bonnyrigg via Cockpen. Johnnie Dods, brother-in-law of the owner, worked there as a mechanic for many years. Known as a character, he never wore socks because he'd been told it would help his sweaty feet! The picture here was taken in the early 1960s and the firm closed down about ten years later. The partly demolished building is now home to Scotia Cars.

The tracks (photographed here at Eskbank Station) have been removed with the line now part of the Dalkeith to Penicuik cycle-way/walk-way.

Work started on the Dalhousie to Edinburgh line in 1827. It opened in 1831 and for three years serviced the pits at a huge loss, until a contractor called Michael Fox approached the company with the idea of an extension to Dalkeith for passengers. The service was hugely successful, carrying an estimated 300,000 passengers each year. It was known as the 'Innocent Railway' because it wasn't involved in a single accident during its first thirteen years of operation. The line was taken over by the North British Railway in 1844 and was in use for more than another 100 years. However, Dalkeith station was closed to passengers in 1942 although the line continued to carry freight until the mid-60s. In 1947 a soup factory was set up in the old Air Raid Post and part of the railway station building. The site was eventually taken over by Scottish Omnibuses Ltd (Eastern Scottish) who built a bus station and garage there.

Taken at the turn of the twentieth century, these photographs of Scott's Close and Moffat's Close show the narrow corridors crammed in between the main streets that allowed infectious diseases of the time to spread so easily. The closes got little light or air and fell into disrepair, the staircases in particular being noted as hazardous. Despite this, they are remembered as friendly places to live where there was a real sense of community. Scott's Close was eventually widened to form Duke Street as part of the slum clearance programme started in the 1930s during which 780 odd homes were condemned. It was previously the site of a thirteenth century church whose remains were discovered by builders developing the area in 1881; evidence that earlier Dalkeithians were just as negligent of their heritage as some twentieth century guardians could be.

16566   MOFFAT'S CLOSE.   OLD DALKEITH.

16569 BACK STREET.　　　　OLD DALKEITH.

Back Street, situated south of High Street, has now been renamed St Andrew's Street, and when this picture was taken in 1908 it was famous for providing Dalkeith's liquid refreshments. Established in 1789, the Dalkeith Brewery Company eventually expanded to cover both sides of the street. The site had its own artesian well, providing water for beers such as the potent Dalkeith Screwtop, and in the 1950s was still using the original engine to draw off supplies. The brewery eventually became part of Tennant Caledonian. During the 1950s the concern lost its Brewer and when he was not replaced both the beer and the business were said to suffer. In 1955 the brewery was sold and went through a winding down process. After a fire on the premises, the buildings were demolished in the late 1960s.

Davidson's pub (better known as the Red Lion) was on High Street. Advertised in its window are the latest offerings from nearby cinemas. The Picture Palace was in operation in Dalkeith around 1912, along with other venues which sometimes showed films such as the Foresters' Hall. By the 1940s the cinemas in the town were the Playhouse and the Pavilion, which in April 1939 were screening *Snow White and the Seven Dwarfs* and Hitchcock's *The Lady Vanishes* respectively. A brief article in the *Advertiser* in the same year advertised a propaganda film to be shown in town called *The Warning*. This was to increase the number of volunteers from Dalkeith into the Mid-Lothian National Service since a previous recruitment drive hadn't had much success.

As well as being the approach to the Palace, this wide stretch of High Street (10.5 yards wider than Princes Street, as the sign waspishly points out) was the site of the old grain market. Grain dealers came into Dalkeith from Mid- and East Lothian, Selkirk and Peebles each Thursday, with sometimes as many as five hundred carts lining the street. Pre-1581 markets were held on Sundays but this breach of the Sabbath was subsequently banned by an Act of Parliament. There were also bi-annual 'Hiring Fairs' for farm labourers held in Dalkeith although by the 1950s this tradition had died out and was only remembered in gala events going by the same name. On the far left of this picture is the Cross Keys Hotel, with the old jail to the right of it.

Taken in 1906, this picture of High Street shows customers queuing for the steam bus.

The street decorations and gawkers in this picture of High Street suggest that it may have been taken during a royal visit. Certainly, there was a procession of some kind happening, going by the focused gaze of the spectators. The first shop on the left, which seems to be some kind of gentleman's outfitters, is now home to a branch of the Abbey National. Next to it is a bakers, now a pet shop. No.31, formerly George McDougal's drapers, currently houses Curry's electrical goods shop.

FISH RESTAURANT.

HIGH STREET, DALKEITH.

High Street, photographed from the close between numbers 31 and 39. The nearest building on the left (formerly Smith's Restaurant) and the building adjoining it, have been demolished and replaced by Woolworths. Directly beyond them stood the Brush Factory, whose sign can be made out between the second and third floor windows. Established in the late eighteenth century, it was one of the oldest industries in Dalkeith, producing all manner of brushes, particularly those used for paper-making. In the 1950s the *Third Statistical Account* noted that 'Bristles made from the new synthetic fibre known as Nylon, are used to some extent.' Dalkeith's Congregational Church, visible near the middle of the right-hand side of the picture, made way for a branch of Boots the Chemist in the 1970s.

32

High Street, 1930s. Dalkeith High Street housed two important buildings, the old jail and the corn exchange. The latter (located at the very bottom of the street on the right) was built by public subscription in 1854 as a venue for the various markets going on in the town. A century later it was too big for its original purpose and was used instead for public meetings, later being leased as the Empress Ballroom. The old jail is still standing, but was not built in 1648 as the date over the doorway states! Accommodation comprised a weigh-house (for market days) and a cell for offenders on the ground floor. Above these were a court room and a prison. Offences were mostly pretty tame, although crime and punishment was not always so mild in the past. In the mid-1600s six people were burned at the stake in Dalkeith for witchcraft, and in 1661 it was even thought necessary for a justice-depute to visit Dalkeith weekly to check up on the witchcraft situation!

HIGH STREET. DALKEITH.

This 1930s picture shows Spier's Auctioneers in the foreground on the right. Its easy to see why Burns Fountain – bang in the middle of the road at the junction of High Street and South Street – was removed in 1968 as a traffic hazard. The fountain was erected on the centenary of the bard's death using funds raised by the local Burns Club. A statuette within it was stolen and the fountain's shell now stands in Kings Park. Cobbie's Bus stands on the right hand side of the street.

High Street looking out from the corner of North Wynd. The business on the left-hand corner, now the Bank of Scotland, became the Red Lion pub while the large tenement block on the right incorporating the 'Cheapest Boot Shop in the County' has totally gone. North Wynd held some important businesses including the Dalkeith Advertiser and a brass foundry. The latter was established in 1854 and survived until the 1950s at least. The company had its own electricity plant and used the old manse of the Relief Church as a store.

HIGH STREET, DALKEITH

D 7832

The same stretch of road as on page 32, photographed in 1961. Woolworths appears next to the Brush Factory which closed during the 60s, with part of the old works eventually making way for extensions to Woollies. There is a Bedford lorry in the distance, and a Morris van and Austin Cambridge on the right.

All of the street paraphernalia keeping the fountain company in this early 1960s shot of High Street has gone. Shrubs and signposts have been cleared away and the A68 is now tagged for Jedburgh. The block on the left was home to Baird's Mens Clothing shop and has now gone. Manchester House, on the right, was a drapers selling towels and bedding. Steeles, to the right of it, has changed hands but is still a jewellers.

16567 PARISH CHURCH.   DALKEITH.

Part of St. Nicholas's Parish Church on the High Street dates back to the fifteenth century, and it is thought that there was once an even earlier chapel on the site. In 1650 Cromwell paid a visit to Scotland making Dalkeith his headquarters. He housed the English Guard and their horses in the parish church, apparently making the minister of the time too feart to give sermons. The ruined section, formerly an apse containing a stone effigy of James Douglas (the first Earl of Morton) and his wife amongst others, is still in the same state today as it was when this picture was taken in 1904. It was sealed off after the Reformation as a 'monument of idolatry' with the roof collapsing due to neglect around 1770. Although it's a pity for any building to fall apart, its ruinous state gives the church an air of history that might be missing otherwise. The tenement block behind on the right was demolished in the late 1930s.

These children are celebrating Queen Elizabeth's coronation in 1953 – they look as if they are waiting for someone important and she may have passed through the town at this time.

Post Office, Dalkeith.

Dalkeith Post Office, as seen in this 1906 picture, has totally gone. The Buccleuch Street site is now the entrance to a car park while the small ironmongers beside it has become a coffee shop. As far back as 1837 when the post master was one Robert Gray, the post office was located in High Street. It later moved to Robertson's Close before relocating to Buccleuch Street (once called Henry's Row) in 1902. The final move to Eskbank Road was made in 1974. Incidentally, Dalkeith Palace Library was the location of a great stamp-collecting find in 1945. A block of 48 2*d.* blue stamps printed almost a century before was discovered and sold for the huge sum of 6,000 guineas.

This Co-operative drapery department was at No.5 Newmills Road. It is now Jay Dees Beauty Salon which has also acquired the space next door on the right.

South Street, Dalkeith.

The entire right-hand side of South Street was demolished to provide space for the Jarnac Court shopping centre. Previously two drapers, Wight and Gray, occupied the shops near the front of the picture on the right. The building in the left foreground, once Wilsons the saddler, is still standing as is the tenement block beside it. In the distance the white gable end of the Old Meal Market Inn is visible, as well as the 'People's Palace' Co-op building.

Meetings on women's rights were taking place in Dalkeith as early as 1884. One in 1913 at the Burn's fountain (perhaps the one pictured here) became the subject of more than usual controversy when a gun-powder bomb was discovered in St Mary's Church a few days later. Church bombings were one of the more extreme suffragette tactics but this one failed – if it was in fact planted by them – since the fuse burnt out too early. However, nearby Whitekirk Church was burned down in a similar attack. Use of such extreme measures is hardly surprising considering what women of the time had to put up with. When there were rumours that female candidates would stand for council election in 1907, Dr Mitchell, a male contender, displayed his true chauvinist colours arguing that women couldn't be trusted with power because they would waste council time with snowball fights and picnics. It sounds to me like he was running scared!

TRAVELLERS REST, DALKEITH.

When this photograph was taken, normal pubs closed on a Sunday because of the licensing laws. A loophole in the laws allowed travellers the right to alcoholic refreshment and so pubs sprung up in isolated areas to take advantage of this.

A Gothenburg was a style of public house run on principles designed to put it out of business! Originally a Swedish movement, the ideas were imported to the East of Scotland by people involved in sea trade with the Baltic. The idea was to set up a liquor house and use most of the profits (dividends were restricted to 5 per cent) for a variety of lofty 'good works'. These included enhancing the town, improving social conditions, and ultimately preventing drunkenness. These members, drinking selflessly for the good of Dalkeith, were photographed as part of the annual parade to raise funds for the Edinburgh Royal Infirmary. The company built Dalkeith's Black Bull pub, but strangely there are no records of consequent improvements to the town. In the 1930s the Gothenburg constitution changed to the extent that it lost popularity with both members and the public, resulting in the movement dying out.

Lugton Village, Dalkeith.

Picturesque Lugton Village was once a separate barony in its own right. It belonged to the Douglas's, who acquired it, along with the Barony of Dalkeith, by marriage into the Graham family. Later in its history it had a rather divided and confused ownership, although it was part of a 1642 charter presented to the Duchess of Buccleuch. Lugton was the birthplace of Robert Smith who went on to become an important builder and architect when he emigrated to Philadelphia around 1747. The picture here was taken in August 1906 – the large ivy-covered building on the right has since gone.

Woodburn House stood on the South Esk and in 1824 was the residence of one Mr James Wilson, who married Isabella Keith. The couple were both naturalists and together wrote many of the natural history articles in the *Encyclopaedia Britannica*. The house has since gone, the area taken over to build the Woodburn scheme. Miners brought in from Lanarkshire were given houses here and around 1950 one hundred and fifty were moved in.

ESKBANK GIRLS SCHOOL,

HOCKEY TEAM.

I haven't been able to uncover much about the adventures of Eskbank Girls' School hockey team except that in 1912 they thrashed Brunstone (a Portobello team) 3:1 in Dalkeith's public park! Perhaps someone recognises the players?

Workers at Newmills Sawmill. This postcard was posted by a son of the owner with the message reading as follows: 'Here is a photo of Father's workmen. There are 35 here (there should be 36 but one was off at the time) and 2 are left out as the postcard is not big enough to hold them all. Father is in the centre – the one with the felt hat on and the paper in his hand. The inside and outside foremen are on either side of him while my brother (who is youngest apprentice at present) is at the end of the 2nd row. I have put a cross above him to let you know.'

St John's Free Church, built in 1844. From 1912 the building served as a cinema, finally being demolished in 1939 to make way for a new Playhouse Cinema. This latter building was eventually taken over by the Corner Pocket Snooker Centre. The Royal British Legion stands on its left, while the building on the right has since become home to Carlton Bingo.

The Harrow Hotel, still standing, appears in the middle left of this 1890s photograph of Eskbank Road. Further down the street on the other side is the Buck's Head pub, now a Chinese restaurant. The two-storey tenement in the right foreground was once home to Halls the Butcher, and the pokey-hat tenement is now council offices.

Taken in May 1908, this picture and the one opposite show the gymnastic team of the Working Lads Institute performing two tableaux. This would have been a presentation at the annual class social and prize-giving. The gymnastic team also competed widely with rivals in the local area.